124 Sales Quotes for Success

How to Unlock the Profits Hidden In You!

Published by: Argon Media, LLC
1026 28th St Suite 9926
Wyoming, MI 49519

Exclusive Bonus Resource for Readers of 124 Sales Quotes For Success

✔ Discover the 4 Steps to Winning Everyday in Every Way in your sales and business life!

✔ Learn how you can make money consistently and effortlessly even in this economy.

✔ Get insider secrets to attracting and keeping your soul mate happy!

Visit http://goo.gl/sQZg9n to claim your above FREE exclusive bonus content.

Table of Contents

Publisher's Notes

Dedication

Life's a Performance

Opportunity Abounds

Improvement is Essential

Time is Fleeting

Ability Is Overrated

The Recipe for Success

About The Author

Publisher's Notes

Dedication

Know ye not that they which run in a race run all, but that one receiveth the prize? So run, that ye may obtain.

~ I Corinthians 9:24 KJV

Life's a Performance

"I have missed more than 9,000 shots in my career. I have lost almost 300 games. On 26 occasions I have been entrusted to take the game winning shot... and I missed. I have failed over and over and over again in my life. And that's precisely why I succeed." ~ Michael Jordan

"When we let freedom ring, when we let it ring from every village and every hamlet, from every state and every city, we will be able to speed up that day when all of God's children, black men and white men, Jews and Gentiles, Protestants and Catholics, will be able to join hands and sing in the words of that old Negro spiritual, ' Free at last! Free at last! Thank God Almighty, we are free at last! ' " ~ Reverand Martin Luther King Jr.

"It's simply a matter of doing what you do best and not worrying about what the other fellow is going to do."~ John R. Amos

"There are glimpses of heaven to us in every act, or thought, or word, that raises us above ourselves." ~ Arthur P. Stanley

"Time = Life. Therefore, waste your time and waste of your life, or master your time and master your life."~ Alan Lakein

"Every child has great ambitions. As she grows, she is bombarded by negative suggestions -- you can't do this; you can't do that; be careful; look for security, and so on. Year by year, she experiences the "realities" of life, and her ambitions fade away. Figuratively speaking, most children die by the time they reach their adulthood." ~ Shall Sinha

"The world cares very little about what a man or woman knows; it is what a man or woman is able to do that counts."~ Booker T. Washington

"If you have a great ambition, take as big a step as possible in the direction of fulfilling it. The step may only be a tiny one, but trust that it may be the largest one possible for now."

~ Mildred Mcafee

"Sometimes only a change of viewpoint is needed to convert a tiresome duty into an interesting opportunity."~ Alberta Flanders

"Believe in yourself! Have faith in your abilities! Without a humble but reasonable confidence in your own powers you cannot be successful or happy." ~ Norman Vincent Peale

"Determine what specific goal you want to achieve. Then dedicate yourself to its attainment with unswerving singleness of purpose, the trenchant zeal of a crusader."~ Paul J. Meyer

"By believing passionately in something that still does not exist, we create it. The nonexistent is whatever we have not sufficiently desired." ~ Nikos Kazantzakis

"Time is at once the most valuable and the most perishable of all our possessions."~ John Randolph

"The only thing that stands between a man/woman and what he wants from life is often merely the will to try it and the faith to believe that it is possible." ~ Richard M. DeVos

"The idea is to make decisions and act on them -- to decide what is important to accomplish, to decide how something can best be accomplished, to find time to work at it and to get it done."~ Karen Kakascik

"If you don't change your beliefs, your life will be like this forever. Is that good news?" ~ Dr. Robert Anthony

"How hard it is, sometimes, to trust the evidence of one's senses! How reluctantly the mind consents to reality."~ Norman Douglas

"All the works of man have their origin in creative fantasy. What right have we then to deprecate imagination." ~ Carl Jung

"We all have ability. The difference is how we use it."~ Stevie Wonder

"Imagination grows by exercise, and contrary to common belief, is more powerful in the mature than in the young." ~ Sir Paul McCartney

Opportunity Abounds

"Wherever there is danger, there lurks opportunity; whenever there is opportunity, there lurks danger. The two are inseparable. They go together."~ Earl Nightingale

"It is usually the imagination that is wounded first, rather than the heart; it being much more sensitive." ~ Henry David Thoreau

"A strong positive mental attitude will create more miracles than any wonder drug."~ Patricia Neal

"I never hit a shot, not even in practice, without having a very sharp, in-focus picture of it in my head. First I see the ball where I want it to finish, nice and white and sitting up high on the bright green grass. Then the scene quickly changes, and I see the ball going there: its path, trajectory, and shape, even its behavior on landing. Then there is a sort of fade-out, and the next scene shows me making the kind of swing that will turn the previous images into reality." ~ Jack Nicklaus

"Reality leaves a lot to the imagination."~ John Lennon

"Imagination is the beginning of creation. You imagine what you desire; you will what you imagine; and at last you create what you will." ~ George Bernard Shaw

"Leadership is the wise use of power. Power is the capacity to translate intention into reality and sustain it."~ Warren Bennis

"First comes thought; then organization of that thought into ideas and plans; then transformation of those plans into reality. The beginning, as you will observe, is in your imagination." ~ Napoleon Hill

"If you're climbing the ladder of life, you go rung by rung, one step at a time. Don't look too far up, set your goals high but take one step at a time. Sometimes you don't think you're progressing until you step back and see how high you've really gone."~ Donny Osmond

"I noticed an almost universal trait among Super Achievers, and it was what I call Sensory Goal Vision. These people knew what they wanted out of life, and they could sense it multi-dimensionally before they ever had it. They could not only see it, but also taste it, smell it, and imagine the sounds and emotions associated with it. They pre-lived it before they had it. And the sharp, sensory vision became a powerful driving force in their lives." ~ Stephen Devore

"Whenever you're in conflict with someone, there is one factor that can make the difference between damaging your relationship and deepening it. That factor is attitude."~ Timothy Bentley

"My face is set, my gait is fast, my goal is Heaven, my road is narrow, my way is rough, my companions are few, my guide is reliable, my mission is clear. I cannot be bought, compromised, detoured, lured away, turned back, diluted, or delayed. I will not flinch in the face of sacrifice, hesitate in the presence of adversity, negotiate... at the table of the enemy, ponder at the pool of popularity, or meander in a maze of mediocrity. I won't give up, shut up, let up, or slow up."~ Robert Moorehead

Improvement is Essential

"There's only one corner of the universe you can be certain of improving, and that's your own self."~ Aldous Huxley

"Success is the sum of small efforts, repeated day in and day out..."~ Robert Collier

"All great masters are chiefly distinguished by the power of adding a second, a third, and perhaps a fourth step in a continuous line. Many a man/woman had taken the first step. With every additional step you enhance immensely the value of your first." ~ Ralph Waldo Emerson

"Striving for excellence motivates you; striving for perfection is demoralizing."~ Harriet Braiker

"You can do what you want to do, accomplish what you want to accomplish, attain any reasonable objective you may have in mind -- not all of a sudden, perhaps not in one swift and sweeping act of achievement -- but you can do it gradually, day by day and play by play, if you want to do it, if you work to do it, over a sufficiently long period of time." ~ William E. Holler

"In life, as in football, you won't go far unless you know where the goalposts are."~ Arnold H. Glasgow

"You can do what you want to do, accomplish what you want to accomplish, attain any reasonable objective you may have in mind -- not all of a sudden, perhaps not in one swift and sweeping act of achievement -- but you can do it gradually, day by day and play by play, if you want to do it, if you work to do it, over a sufficiently long period of time." ~ William E. Holler

"People never improve unless they look to some standard or example higher or better than themselves."~ Tryon Edwards

"The quality of a person's life is in direct proportion to their commitment to excellence, regardless of their chosen field of endeavor." ~ Vince Lombardi

"We can tell our values by looking at our checkbook stubs."~ Gloria Steinem

"If you want to take your mission in life to the next level, if you're stuck and you don't know how to rise, don't look outside yourself. Look inside. Don't let your fears keep you mired in the crowd. Abolish your fears and raise your commitment level to the point of no return, and I guarantee you that the Champion Within will burst forth to propel you toward victory." ~ Bruce Jenner

"The principle is competing against yourself. It's about self-improvement, about being better than you were the day before."~ Steve Young

"Having once decided to achieve a certain task, achieve it at all costs of tedium and distaste. The gain in self-confidence of having accomplished a tiresome labor is immense. " ~ Thomas A. Bennett

"Life is 10 percent what you make it and 90 percent how you take it."~ Irving Berlin

"Life affords no higher pleasure than that of surmounting difficulties, passing from one step of success to another, forming new wishes and seeing them gratified." ~ Samuel Johnson

"Excellence is doing ordinary things extraordinarily well."~ John W. Gardner

"Someone has defined genius as intensity of purpose: the ability to do, the patience to wait. Put these together and you have achievement." ~ Leo J. Muir

"Whether you think you can or whether you think you can't, you're right!"~ Henry Ford

"Trust yourself. Create the kind of self that you will be happy to live with all your life. Make the most of yourself by fanning the tiny, inner sparks of possibility into flames of achievement." ~ Foster C. McClellan

"When we are motivated by goals that have deep meaning, by dreams that need completion, by pure love that needs expressing, then we truly live life."~ Greg Anderson

"I hope that my achievements in life shall be these -- that I will have fought for what was right and fair, that I will have risked for that which mattered, and that I will have given help to those who were in need... and that I will have left the earth a better place for what I've done and who I've been." ~ C. Hoppe

"Big jobs usually go to the men who prove their ability to outgrow small ones."~ Ralph Waldo Emerson

"I hope that my achievements in life shall be these -- that I will have fought for what was right and fair, that I will have risked for that which mattered, and that I will have given help to those who were in need... and that I will have left the earth a better place for what I've done and who I've been." ~ C. Hoppe

"Neither can the wave that has passed by be recalled, nor the hour which has passed return again."~ Ovid

"My mother drew a distinction between achievement and success. She said that achievement is the knowledge that you have studied and worked hard and done the best that is in you. Success is being praised by others. That is nice but not as important or satisfying. Always aim for achievement and forget about success." ~ Helen Hayes

"It's how we spend our time here and now, that really matters. If you are fed up with the way you have come to interact with time, change it."~ Wieder Marcia

"Opportunities multiply as they are seized, they die when neglected." ~ John Wicker

Time is Fleeting

"Time is the most valuable thing a man can spend."~ Laertius Diogenes

"Wherever we look upon this earth, the opportunities take shape within the problems." ~ Nelson Rockefeller

"It's not hard to make decisions when you know what your values are."~ Roy Disney

"When you feel that you have reached the end and that you cannot go one step further, when life seems to be drained of all purpose: What a wonderful opportunity to start all over again, to turn over a new page." ~ Eileen Caddy

"It's how you deal with failure that determines how you achieve success."~ David Feherty

"Don't wait for extraordinary opportunities. Seize common occasions and make them great. Weak men/women wait for opportunities; strong men/women make them." ~ Orison Swett Marden

"Opportunities are usually disguised as hard work, so most people don't recognize them."~ Ann Landers

"What is opportunity, and when does it knock? It never knocks. You can wait a whole lifetime, listening, hoping, and you will hear no knocking. None at all. You are opportunity, and you must knock on the door leading to your destiny. You prepare yourself to recognize opportunity, to pursue and seize opportunity as you develop the strength of your personality, and build a self-image with which you are able to live -- with your self-respect alive and growing." ~ Maxwell Maltz

"If at first you don't succeed; you are running about average." ~ M. H. Alderson

"A good deal happens in a man's life that he isn't responsible for. Fortunate openings occur; but it is safe to remember that such "breaks" are occurring all the time, and other things being equal, the advantage goes to the man or woman who is ready." ~ Lawrence Downs

"The people who get on in this world are the people who get up and look for the circumstances they want, and, if they can't find them, make them." ~ George Bernard Shaw

"The sad truth is that opportunity doesn't knock twice. You can put things off until tomorrow but tomorrow may never come. Where will you be a few years down the line. Will it be everything you dreamed of. We seal our fate with the choices we make, but don't give a second thought to the chances we take." ~ Gloria Estefan

"The history of the world is full of men who rose to leadership, by sheer force of self-confidence, bravery and tenacity." ~ Mahatma Gandhi

"Adversity? When you come to a roadblock, take a detour." ~ Mary Kay Ash

Ability Is Overrated

"Ability is what you're capable of doing. Motivation determines what you do. Attitude determines how well you do it."~ Lou Holtz

"We acquire the strength we have overcome."? ~Ralph Waldo Emerson

"Skill in the art of communication is crucial to a leader's success. He can accomplish nothing unless he can communicate effectively." ~ Norman Allen

"If you break your neck, if you have nothing to eat, if your house is on fire, then you got a problem. Everything else is inconvenience." ~Robert Fulghum

"Without goals, and plans to reach them, you are like a ship that has set sail with no destination." ~ Fitzhugh Dodson

"If we study the lives of great men and women carefully and unemotionally we find that, invariably, greatness was developed, tested and revealed through the darker periods of their lives. One of the largest tributaries of the RIVER OF GREATNESS is always the STREAM OF ADVERSITY." ~ Cavett Robert

"The reality of life is that your perceptions -- right or wrong -- influence everything else you do. When you get a proper perspective of your perceptions, you may be surprised how many other things fall into place." ~ Roger Birkman

"If we study the lives of great men and women carefully and unemotionally we find that, invariably, greatness was developed, tested and revealed through the darker periods of their lives. One of the largest tributaries of the RIVER OF GREATNESS is always the STREAM OF ADVERSITY." ~ Cavett Robert

"I've always felt it was not up to anyone else to make me give my best." ~ Akeem Olajuwon

"Things don't go wrong and break your heart so you can become bitter and give up. They happen to break you down and build you up so you can be all that you were intended to be." ~ Charles "Tremendous" Jones

"Money will come to you when you are doing the right thing." ~ Michael Phillips

"Trials, temptations, disappointments—all these are helps instead of hindrances, if one uses them rightly. They not only test the fiber of character but strengthen it. Every conquering temptation represents a new fund of moral energy. Every trial endured and weathered in the right spirit makes a soul nobler and stronger than it was before." ~ James Buckham

"Successful people are successful because they form the habits of doing those things that failures don't like to do."~ Albert Gray

"Trials, temptations, disappointments—all these are helps instead of hindrances, if one uses them rightly. They not only test the fiber of character but strengthen it. Every conquering temptation represents a new fund of moral energy. Every trial endured and weathered in the right spirit makes a soul nobler and stronger than it was before." ~ James Buckham

"Don't tell me how hard you work. Tell me how much you get done."~ James Ling

"Without passion man/woman is a mere latent force and possibility, like the flint which awaits the shock of the iron before it can give forth its spark." ~ Henri Frederic Amiel

"The beginning is the most important part of the work." ~ Plato

" Life is change. Growth is optional. Choose wisely. " ~ Karen Kaiser Clark

"Nature arms each man with some faculty which enables him to do easily some feat impossible to any other." ~ Ralph Waldo Emerson

"For every mountain there is a miracle." ~ Robert H. Schuller

"People wait for opportunity to come along...yet it is there every morning." ~ Dennis the Menace

"For a long time it seemed to me that real life was about to begin, but there was always some obstacle in the way. Something had to be got through first, some unfinished business; time still to be served, a debt to be paid. Then life would begin. At last it dawned on me that these obstacles were my life." ~ Bette Howland

"Motivation is like food for the brain. You cannot get enough in one sitting. It needs continual and regular top up's." ~ Peter Davies

"Obstacles are necessary for success... as in all careers of importance, victory comes only after many struggles and countless defeats. Yet each struggle, each defeat, sharpens your skills and strengths, your courage and your endurance, your ability and your confidence and thus each obstacle is a comrade-in-arms forcing you to become better... or quit. Each rebuff is an opportunity to move forward; turn away from them, avoid them, and you throw away your future." ~ Og Mandino

"There are no menial jobs, only menial attitudes." ~ William John Bennett

"Much as we may wish to make a new beginning, some part of us resists doing so as though we were making the first step toward disaster." ~ William Bridges

"Executive ability is deciding quickly and getting somebody else to do the work." ~ John G. Pollard

"Much as we may wish to make a new beginning, some part of us resists doing so as though we were making the first step toward disaster." ~ William Bridges

The Recipe for Success

"The man who gets the most satisfactory results is not always the man with the most brilliant single mind, but rather the man who can best coordinate the brains and talents of his associates." ~ W. Alton Jones

"What is the recipe for successful achievement? To my mind there are just four essential ingredients: Choose a career you love, give it the best there is in you, seize your opportunities, and be a member of the team."~ Benjamin F. Fairless

"If you will call your troubles experiences, and remember that every experience develops some latent force within you, you will grow vigorous and happy, however adverse your circumstances may seem to be." ~ John R. Miller

"If, before going to bed every night, you will tear a page from the calendar, and remark, "there goes another day of my life, never to return," you will become time conscious." ~ A. B. Zu Tavern

"Some men/women have thousands of reasons why they cannot do what they want to, when all they need is one reason why they can." ~ Willis Whitney

"Lost wealth may be replaced by industry, lost knowledge by study, lost health by temperance or medicine, but lost time is gone forever."~ Samuel Smiles

"Attitudes are the forerunners of conditions." ~ Eric Butterworth

"There is great treasure there behind our skull and this is true about all of us. This little treasure has great, great powers, and I would say we only have learnt a very, very small part of what it can do." ~ Isaac Bashevis Singer

"Your living is determined not so much by what life brings to you as by the attitude you bring to life; not so much by what happens to you as by the way your mind looks at what happens." ~ John Homer Miller

"Your goals, minus your doubts, equal your reality." ~ Ralph Marston

"Our attitudes control our lives. Attitudes are a secret power working twenty-four hours a day, for good or bad. It is of paramount importance that we know how to harness and control this great force." ~ Tom Blandi

"A test of what is real is that it is hard and rough. Joys are found in it, not pleasure. What is pleasant belongs to dreams." ~ Simone Weil

"People should know what you stand for. They should also know what you won't stand for." ~ Author Unknown

"Whatever you do, don't do it halfway."~ Bob Beamon

"People should know what you stand for. They should also know what you won't stand for." ~ Author Unknown

"The biggest difference between time and space is that you can't reuse time."~
Merrick Furst

"Tell me what gives a man or woman their greatest pleasure (values) and I'll tell
you their philosophy of life." ~ Dale Carnegie

"Success is not forever and failure isn't fatal." ~ Don Shula

"We can tell our values by looking at our checkbook stubs." ~ Gloria Steinem

"One important key to success is self-confidence. An important key to self-
confidence is preparation." ~ Arthur Ashe

"All sciences are now under the obligation to prepare the ground for the future
task of the philosopher, which is to solve the problem of value, to determine the
true hierarchy of values." ~ Friedrich Nietzsche

"Leaders aren't born, they are made. And they are made just like anything else,
through hard work. And that's the price we'll have to pay to achieve that goal, or
any goal." ~ Vince Lombardi

"It's not hard to make decisions when you know what your values are." ~ Roy
Disney

"Ability is of little account without opportunity."~ Napoleon Bonaparte

Try not to become a man/woman of success but rather try to become a man of value." ~ Albert Einstein

"Nobody motivates today's workers. If it doesn't come from within, it doesn't come. Fun helps remove the barriers that allow people to motivate themselves."~ Herman Cain

"If you do not feel yourself growing in your work and your life broadening and deepening, if your task is not a perpetual tonic to you, you have not found your place." ~ Orison Swett Marden

"Watch your thoughts; they become words. Watch your words; they become actions. Watch your actions; they become habits. Watch your habits; they become character. Watch your character; it becomes your destiny."-- Frank Outlaw

"People rarely succeed unless they have fun in what they are doing." ~ Dale Carnegie

"Our business in life is not to get ahead of others, but to get ahead of ourselves -- to break our own records, to outstrip our yesterday by our today."~ Stewart B. Johnson

"There are two freedoms—the false, where a man is free to do what he likes; the true, where he is free to do what he ought." ~ Charles Kingsley

"It is those who have this imperative demand for the best in their natures, and who will accept nothing short of it, that holds the banners of progress, that set the standards, the ideals, for others."~ Orison Swett Marden

"Freedom is not an ideal, it is not even a protection, if it means nothing more than freedom to stagnate, to live without dreams, to have no greater aim than a second car and another television set." ~ Adlai E. Stevenson

"Our attitudes control our lives. Attitudes are a secret power working twenty-four hours a day, for good or bad. It is of paramount importance that we know how to harness and control this great force."~ Tom Blandi

"The only freedom which deserves the name is that of pursuing our own good, in our own way, so long as we do not attempt to deprive others of theirs, or impede their efforts to obtain it." ~ John Stuart Mill

"There are only 3 colors, 10 digits, and 7 notes; its what we do with them that's important."~ Ruth Ross

"When people talk of the freedom of writing, speaking or thinking I cannot choose but laugh. No such thing ever existed. No such thing now exists; but I hope it will exist. But it must be hundreds of years after you and I shall write and speak no more." ~ John Quincy Adams

"The world cares very little about what a man or woman knows; it is what a man or woman is able to do that counts."~ Booker T. Washington

"Freedom know this, that every man/woman is free To choose his life and what he'll be. For this eternal truth is given, God will force no man to heaven. He'll call, persuade, direct aright, Bless with wisdom, love, and light; In nameless ways be good and kind, But never force the human mind."~ William C. Clegg

"Each experience through which we pass operates ultimately for our good. This is a correct attitude to adopt and we must be able to see it in that light."~ Raymond Holliwell

"It has never been, and never will be, easy work! But the road that is built in hope is more pleasant to the traveler than the road built in despair, even though they both lead to the same destination." ~Marion Zimmer Bradley

"It has always been my belief that a man should do his best, regardless of how much he receives for his services, or the number of people he may be serving or the class of people served."~ Napoleon Hill

www.ingramcontent.com/pod-product-compliance
Lightning Source LLC
Chambersburg PA
CBHW051226170526
45166CB00005B/2064